THEN & NOW

MONROE TOWNSHIP AND JAMESBURG

Opposite: **THE FIRST NATIONAL BANK OF JAMESBURG, C. 1925.** The First National Bank of Jamesburg received its charter on February 27, 1864. It was the 288th institution of its kind to be chartered by the United States government. Built around 1864, it was then located in the village of Jamesburg, in the township of Monroe (Jamesburg was not yet an independent borough). Bank director William H. Brooks is standing on the left, and a Mr. Gunson is on the right. Today the site is the Dunkin' Donuts parking lot.

THEN & NOW

MONROE TOWNSHIP
AND JAMESBURG

John D. Katerba

*This book is dedicated to my beautiful wife, Josephine,
and to my sons, Joseph Daniel and Christopher John Katerba.
Thank you all for your continued support and patience
over the five years it took to complete this book.*

Library of Congress control number: 2007924459

Published by Arcadia Publishing
Charleston SC, Chicago IL, Portsmouth NH, San Francisco CA

Printed in the United States of America

For all general information contact Arcadia Publishing at:
Telephone 843-853-2070
Fax 843-853-0044
E-mail sales@arcadiapublishing.com
For customer service and orders:
Toll-Free 1-888-313-2665

Visit us on the Internet at www.arcadiapublishing.com

On the front cover: THE RED TAVERN. One of the earliest recorded structures in Monroe Township was the Red Tavern, built in Colonial times. The first recorded owner was Colonel Jones about 1800. There was a succession of owners after Jones, until 1853 when Samuel Vandenbergh, shown on the porch with his family about 1875, purchased it. At his death, his son James took over management of the business. In 1901, James sold the Red Tavern structure to Enos Mount, who moved it across the street next to his existing store. Construction began on the new Applegarth Hotel in the summer of 1901. In 1914, lightning struck the old Red Tavern, and it was burned to the ground along with the Enos Mount General Store. Presently, the former Applegarth Hotel serves as a restaurant and bar. Jose Martin-Serrano opened Europa at Monroe in May 2006, and it has been serving the community well with quality food and drink. (Author's collection.)

On the back cover: MEMBERS OF THE JAMESBURG FIRE DEPARTMENT. Members of the Jamesburg Fire Department are shown here around 1905 on Forsgate Drive for Decoration Day (Memorial Day). Young Gladys Quinn, holding a pennant that says "Hook and Ladder," is next to her father, Christopher Quinn, the driver. Fred Cole is standing on the left; Jacob Houser is in the center. The man to the right is unidentified. (Author's collection.)

CONTENTS

ACKNOWLEDGMENTS

I would like to thank each and every person who gave their time and effort to make this book possible. Again to Tim Stoessler for his late-night typing and to his wife, Barbara, and kids Joe and Natalie Guidice for their consideration by going to Disney in order to give him the typing time he needed. Thank you to the Jamesburg Historical Society, the Monroe Township Historic Preservation Commission, the Cranbury Historical Society, and most of all to George B. Hausman; without his dedication to collecting photographs, and recording the information with them, this book would not be possible.

I would also like to thank the following people for contributing many of the photographs that make up this second book: Louise Johnson Kerwin, Milt Fischer, Billie and Roy Conover, Art and Peggy Romweber, Roi Taylor, Jamesburg historian Thomas C. Bodall, Maria Nasser, Bill and Janet Schlegel, Josie Chamberlain, Harold Applegate, Kathryn and Charlotte Ely, George and Sue Baker, Don Magian, Ray Murasko, Butch Van Pelt, John M. Tancredi, Jack Abeel, Bea Rogers, Beverly Hobbs, Margaret Daly, Dick and Florence Clayton, Fred Perrine, John Painter, Malcolm and Marcia Kirkpatrick, Gary and Jeff Clayton, and Harold Stillwell.

INTRODUCTION

On February 23, 1838, the council and general assembly of New Jersey, acting on the petition of certain inhabitants of the township of South Amboy, passed an act to set off from the township of South Amboy, in the county of Middlesex, a new township to be called the township of Monroe in honor of Pres. James Monroe. This tract, eight miles long and six miles wide in the southeastern corner of the county, included not only the present Monroe Township but also Jamesburg, Spotswood, Helmetta, and parts of Cranbury and East Brunswick Townships.

This new township was primarily agricultural, a reason for its separation from the increasingly industrial and commercial South Amboy after the Revolutionary War. The first settler who came to Monroe, in 1685, was James Johnstone of Ochiltree, Scotland, who built his home and a sawmill on the Manalapan Brook between Spotswood and Jamesburg. Johnstone was followed by other settlers who came from Scotland, England, Staten Island, and Long Island. Good water was abundant in the Manalapan (meaning "land of good bread") Brook and in the Matchaponix (meaning "land of poor bread") Brook, which met at Spotswood, the first settlement in the area, and flowed into the South River and eventually into Raritan Bay.

A gristmill, sawmill, and blacksmith shop were established in Jamesburg in the early. 1700s. There were other mills, crossroad stores, one-room schoolhouses, distilleries, and taverns in various areas known as Applegarth, Half Acre, Prospect Plains, Union Valley, Old Church, Gravel Hill, Dey Grove, Pleasant Grove, Matchaponix, Mounts Mills, Outcalt, and Texas.

In 1746, David Brainerd, Presbyterian-allied missionary to the Native Americans, established a settlement called Bethel (House of God) on an 80-acre tract in the township in what is now Middlesex County's Thompson Park. Here, under Brainerd's direction, the Native Americans built log houses, a log church, and a school and cultivated English grain, Indian corn, fruit trees, and other crops. In 1760, by New Jersey government order, all Native Americans were moved to a reservation at Brotherton, Burlington County. The site of Bethel was marked with a historical marker by the Monroe Area Historical Association in 1977.

On June 27, 1778, the night before the Battle of Monmouth, Gen. George Washington, his officers, and troops stayed in the Gravel Hill section of Monroe Township. None of the houses used by the officers are still standing, but the locations are known.

The coming of the Camden and Amboy Railroad in 1831 and the Jamesburg and Freehold Agricultural Railroad in 1853, both of which crossed the township, greatly increased the ability of the farmers to get their product to city markets and, in turn, to receive fertilizer, seed, and equipment. Passenger service was also very good with depots in the towns and flag stations along the tracks.

In 1867, the reform school, now the New Jersey Training School, was built in the township. In 1896, Jamesburg becomes a completely independent borough, and in 1905, Bernarr Macfadden founded his short-lived Physical Culture City at Outcalt.

In 1918, Forsgate Farms was established by John A. Forster. It became a successful dairy, fruit, poultry, and ice-cream enterprise, with homes for workers and an outstanding golf course and country club. The farm complex was closed in 1971.

For many years, the township was governed by a three-man township committee that elected its own chairman. Many township officials served long and faithfully. In 1962, the committee membership was increased to five.

On January 1, 1972, the township government, by vote of the people, underwent great change. It was organized under the strong mayor-council plan. Joseph Indyk was the first mayor elected directly by the people. Joseph P. Leo was appointed business administrator. There were many active departments and commissions as the burgeoning township's government became more complex and sophisticated.

In the earliest days of the township committee, it met in a member's home or in a schoolhouse. Official records were kept in private homes. After it was no longer used as a school, the old schoolhouse at Prospect Plains became the town hall, or municipal meeting place. In the 1970s, the schoolhouse on the corner of Schoolhouse Road, which had served as police headquarters, became the administrative office. The present municipal building on Perrineville Road with space for all departments was dedicated on September 27, 1981. In the same complex were built the Public Works Department building and the police headquarters. The township has four fire companies, a first aid squad, and civic and social organizations.

Education has always been important in Monroe Township. When the township was organized in 1838, an amount of $1,500 was immediately appropriated for schools. By 1864, there were 16 one-room schools in the township. In 1936, two consolidated brick elementary schools were opened, the present Barclay Brook and Applegarth Schools. Rapid population growth created the need for building the Woodland, Mill Lake, and Brookside Schools. Currently a new elementary school is set to be built on Applegarth Road.

In January 1974, the first high school in Monroe Township opened its doors, and Monroe was no longer a secondary sending district. In 1979, it became a receiving district for Jamesburg high school pupils. Due to the growing township, a new high school has been approved for construction.

The official symbol of Monroe Township is the "Monroe Oak," a true monarch, which rules majestically on the corner of Prospect Plains Road and Applegarth Road on the property of the Provident Bank. This tree is more than 300 years old, which means it was a sprouting acorn when James Johnstone first came to Monroe. It is registered as one of "Penn's Trees," meaning it was in existence when William Penn landed in America in 1682. In 1974, through the efforts of the late R. Maitland Vandenbergh and the Monroe Area Historical Association, the tree was made the official symbol of the township.

Today Monroe Township is a growing community of close to 40,000 residents and only a scant few farms are still in operation. And while the township has a bright future, residents continue to remember, preserve, and maintain their rich past.

The Monroe Township Historic Preservation Commission is proud to be at the forefront of this initiative. Its members are actively involved in activities that both protect and commemorate the township's history. These include acquiring the Charles Dey farm, which sits on 40 acres, moving the England house to the site in 2004, and other preservation projects.

The Jamesburg Historical Association continues to protect its historical Lakeview House on Buckelew Avenue and hosts many quality historical events throughout the year. Currently Ronald Becker is the association president, and Thomas C. Bodall serves as Jamesburg's official historian.

—Louise Johnson Kerwin, John D. Katerba, and Renee Hobbs

MONROE TOWNSHIP

THE DEBOW FARM, C. 1915. The DeBow Farm was located at Prospect Plains Road where the most southern part of the Rossmoor community is now. From left to right in the photograph is a brand-new Ford Model T touring car, an unidentified vehicle with a 1915 New York license plate, and a very early c. 1910 Franklin automobile. William DeBow can be seen standing next to the Franklin on the right. His wife, Mary, is seated inside the car from New York.

THE PROSPECT PLAINS RAILROAD STATION. November 21, 1831, marked the first movement by steam on a railroad in the state of New Jersey, and possibly the entire country. The original locomotive *John Bull* now resides at the National Museum of American History in Washington, D.C. The first steel T rail was laid near Bordentown in August 1831. Over a year later, on December 17, 1832, the first passengers were transported from Bordentown to South Amboy. The Prospect Plains station, pictured here around 1905, was closed in 1939. The station was located on Public Road just south of the Cranberry's Gourmet Shoppe.

HOME OF MR. AND MRS. GEORGE F. MORSE. Located on Prospect Plains Road, the home of Mr. and Mrs. George F. Morse, seen here around 1915, was later owned by their daughter Bessie Morse. It was said Bessie was a bit of an eccentric. She was a crack shot with a rifle and an avid hunter. It is rumored that a longtime house guest of Bessie's passed away at her home. She took it upon herself to embalm the fellow in the parlor. Across the street at that time was the home of Mr. and Mrs. John W. O'Keefe. On the former O'Keefe property is the resting place of several Revolutionary War soldiers. These soldiers perished on June 27, 1778, from the excessive heat. Today most of the Morse farm has become part of Greenbriar at Whittingham.

ROMWEBER AND SON GENERAL STORE AND POST OFFICE. Located on Public Road, Romweber and Son general store and post office was opened in 1908 by Abijah Applegate. Emil Romweber purchased the store and became postmaster in 1923. At first, the potbellied stove was the only heat at the store, and there was no electricity. Refrigeration had to come from an icebox and light from the kerosene lamp. Electricity came around 1928. Later, in 1955, Emil Romweber retired and his son Arthur took over. Pictured here in 1951, the store closed in 1983 and was reopened in 1987 as the current Cranberry's Gourmet Shoppe.

PROSPECT PLAINS ROAD FACING WEST. On the right, at the time of this *c.* 1915 photograph, is the newly constructed home of R. Maitland Vandenbergh. Years before, on that very spot, stood the original general store. It was built in 1832 by Davison and Stonaker. In 1859, a post office was housed there. In March 1907, fire destroyed the store and post office, and it was reopened where the present-day Cranberry's Gourmet Shoppe is now located. The home at the left was known as the Edwards farm. The white farmhouse in the foreground was built by the Stults family more than a century ago. It is now owned by Hildegard Gross.

THE EDWARDS FARM. The Edwards farm was located on Prospect Plains Road. Across the street from the old R. Maitland Vandenbergh house stood the home of Charles H. Edwards. The poultry boom at the beginning of the 20th century was Edwards's inspiration for inventing a "setting hen," a zinc-lined box filled with sawdust in which the eggs were placed in trays. Water, its temperature regulated by a thermometer, was poured in twice daily. Edwards claimed a 75 percent success rate for his mechanical setting hen. The farmhouse, seen here around 1915, was torn down in June 1994, and the Remsterville Learning Center was built in its place.

THE PROSPECT PLAINS INN AND BAR ROOM. Located at the corner of Prospect Plains and Applegarth Roads, the Prospect Plains Inn and Bar Room was originally built as a residence by William Stults around 1832. It was converted into the Railroad Hotel by Arthur Duding in 1862. Around 1903, Robert R. Vandenbergh and his new bride, Mary, purchased the old hotel, seen here around 1930. On October 9, 1975, the old hotel was razed to make way for a bank. The new bank, Pulawski Savings and Loan, opened the following year in 1976. The building has changed names several times over the years. At one point it was Pulse Savings Bank and then First Savings, and it is presently the Provident Bank.

THE HOME OF D. C. MERSHOW ON PROSPECT PLAINS ROAD. This pristine farm shows up on the 1876 county map as belonging to J. Stults, and in 1898, a map shows it being owned by D. C. Mershow. Later, in the mid-1950s, this farm was owned by Ted Oldzejs. Pictured here around 1915, this farm was later sold and torn down to make way for Rossmoor. Today the Rossmoor maintenance department is located close to where the farm was. Most all the Prospect Plains images in this book were published by Abijah Applegate around 1915. At this time, he was the owner of the Prospect Plains General Store and Post Office.

THE HOME OF WILLIAM H. DEBOW ON PROSPECT PLAINS ROAD, WEST OF THE MERSHOW FARM. At the time of this c. 1915 postcard view, William H. DeBow (born in 1860) and his wife, Mary (born in 1855), lived here at this beautiful farm. William DeBow and Mary (neé Fisher) DeBow were married on January 31, 1884, in Cranbury. They purchased the farm from Charles A. Stults around the late 19th century. An old receipt found from 1920 shows that DeBow was a dealer in fertilizers, seed potatoes, and farm produce. The farm was later sold to Rossmoor and was razed in the 1960s. The farmhouse was located where the old south gate of Rossmoor once was.

THE GEORGE M. DUNCAN FARM. George M. Duncan's farm was the last farm located in Monroe on the south side of Prospect Plains Road, across from the old DeBow farm. Duncan, along with a group of farmers, welcomed the Knights of Pythias with the establishment of the Monroe lodge on February 4, 1892, and 33 members were initiated. Duncan became vice chancellor. The group disbanded in 1897. Later Alex Farr bought the farm and then Carter-Wallace in the 1970s. The Kislin family was the last to occupy the farmhouse, seen here around 1910. It was torn down around 1987. Today the Four Seasons adult community is planned to be built on the site.

CARL DILLER'S HALF ACRE SERVICE STATION. This station, pictured around 1940, was located where the present-day Shell gas station is on the corner of Half-Acre and Prospect Plains Roads. A receipt from the old service station quotes greasing, washing, car accessories, atlas tires, battery service, and rentals. The Texaco Corporation took ownership of the property and razed the old hotel and garage in the mid-1970s. It constructed a redbrick two-bay garage and continued to sell gasoline. In 1987, Jerry and Tracey Noonan took over the service station, and reopened as Jerry Noonan's Half Acre Mobil. That building was demolished in the 1990s, and the present station was built.

WILLIAM WILSON FARM. The Wilson farmhouse was on the north side of Prospect Plains Road. Presently, the south gate of Greenbriar is located here. William Wilson and his wife, Laura Belle (née Davison), were married in the Tennant Church in Monmouth County on March 14, 1889. Soon afterward they came to Monroe Township. Wilson died at the farm in 1937, and his funeral was held at the farmhouse, shown in 1915. In the late 1980s, the Union Valley Corporation built the Whittingham at Monroe Adult Community on this site. After going bankrupt in the early 1990s, U.S. Homes purchased the property and renamed it Greenbriar at Whittingham.

THE CHARLES A. STULTS FARM. Seen here around 1900, this farmhouse rested on a 200-acre farm located on Half-Acre Road. It was located directly across the street from the Monroe Township Municipal Utilities Authority (MUA) water tower. In 1912, Charles A. Stults's son Clifford was riding behind the Morse farm on a horse-drawn corn planter when lightning struck. Both horses were killed instantly. Clifford was unharmed. It was the talk of the town. A postcard company seized the opportunity to photograph the dead horses where they lay. All the buildings were town down in the 1960s. Today this is section C-H of Greenbriar at Whittingham.

THE THOMAS E. MOUNT HOUSE. Presently the Thomas E. Mount house, pictured around 1910, is located on Route 33, north side, one-half mile west of Perrineville Road. One of Mount's children, Ella, was born in the house in 1901. When she was a young girl, a county doctor performed an appendectomy on her by the light of just an oil lamp. The dining room table served as the operating table. When she grew older, she lived in California for a time but returned home to the family farm. She died in the house she was born in on February 16, 1997.

FACING NORTH ON APPLEGARTH ROAD.
On the left, behind the barn and windmill is the Applegarth Hotel, now the Europa at Monroe restaurant, around 1910. The old Red Tavern can be seen in its second location after being moved across the road by Enos Mount in 1901. Next to the tavern is the Mount General Store. The tavern and store were both destroyed by fire in 1914. Today all the barns and outbuildings are long gone. Several ranch-style homes have been built here over the years, including Larks Nursery business where the old Red Tavern and general store once stood.

MONROE TOWNSHIP

APPLEGARTH, WYCOFF MILLS, AND OLD CHURCH ROADS. Facing northeast on Applegarth Road at the "point" around 1910 is the Everingham Wheelwright Shop. It opened the same year Monroe Township was created in 1838. The shop closed around 1928 due to the increasing popularity of the automobile. The old wheelwright shop was torn down in the 1960s and soon after replaced with the present-day block building. Wilbert and Ruth Duncan, the author's grandparents, opened the Applegarth Fabric Shop there. It operated in this location until the mid-1970s, when they relocated their business out to Route 130.

THE RAILROAD HOTEL AT PROSPECT PLAINS. Today the Provident Bank sits on the corner of Prospect Plains Road and Applegarth Road, where the Railroad Hotel (pictured around 1910) once stood. Also on this corner stands one of the area's oldest oak trees. Some have estimated its age at over 400 years. It was incorporated into the township's official symbol in the mid-1970s. Its longevity was threatened in 1972 when the old hotel was sold to Sun Oil Company. The new owners had proposed cutting down the tree and building a gas station. Through the efforts of R. Maitland Vandenbergh and the newly formed Monroe Area Historical Association the tree was spared.

THE FORSGATE INN. Originally built in 1901 by James Vandenbergh, this hotel opened for business as a hotel in October of that same year. The cost for this new state-of-the-art Applegarth Hotel was $5,000. In 1914, James D. Courtney took over and changed the name to Courtney's Hotel. Courtney also ran the distillery at Applegarth. The going rate of his brandy in 1917 was $2.35 per gallon. The old hotel has changed hands over the last half century. Some of the names over the years were Tony Laines, Forsgate Inn (seen here around 1960), the Over the Bridge Inn, Firehouse Eatery, Dominico's, and currently Europa at Monroe, which opened in May 2006.

NO. 87 HALSEY REED ROAD. According to Harold Applegate, his grandparents' former home, pictured in June 1934, was built around 1880. On the 1898 county map, it is shown as being owned by J. Stults. Then, around 1912, Applegate's grandparents George B. Ely and his wife, Mary (née Mount), purchased the home to stay close to his their Clarence Ely. On February 11, 1933, George died suddenly of a heart attack while cranking his Oldsmobile in the driveway. He was 67. Mary Ely stayed in the home until it was sold to Walter Higgins in 1953. Today the home is owned by the nephew of the late Walter Higgins.

THE ELY FARM. Pictured around 1905, this farm was located on Cranbury Station Road. The Stratford at Monroe development is now located where the barns once stood. The farmhouse was on the north side where the homes of the Renaissance at Cranbury Crossings now stand. The farm was purchased in 1894 by George B. Ely and his wife. In 1912, they sold it to his son Clarence Ely and his wife, Lenora (née Applegate). On May 5, 1952, at the age of 63, Clarence died. His wife and two daughters, Kathryn and Charlotte, were left to run the more than 200-acre farm. They sold it in 1955.

TILTON FARMHOUSE AT 225 GRAVEL HILL ROAD. An early deed shows that on April 14, 1873, James Burton sold his 95-acre farm, shown around 1880, to Rosanna Tilton and Rei B. Tilton for $6,000. On August 16, 1932, the Tilton farm came into the spotlight of the national news when 60-year-old William B. Tilton wed 22-year-old Julia Scott, and as part of the very same ceremony, his son Ernest married Julia's 18-year-old sister Celia Scott in a double wedding in Jamesburg. William B. Tilton was quoted after the wedding saying, "The boys in town say I've got the best looking girl in the Scott family. There is a lot of class to her." Henry Tilton (father of William) is shown in this 1880 photograph.

THE HOUSMAN FARM. At 355 Hoffman Station Road, standing from left to right around 1897 are mother Amy, daughters Anna and Cora, and father William Housman. In the buggy sit son-in-law Thomas Forsythe, Emma (née Housman), and her daughter Emma. On June 27, 1778, Gen. George Washington made his headquarters here for the night, while his troops camped on several adjoining farms in the Gravel Hill area. On the morning of the Battle of Monmouth, Washington, while standing on the porch, heard the firing of his Gen. Charles Lee's cannons 10 miles away. He sent immediate orders for his army to move to help assist Lee.

THE TOLLMAN HOUSE. Pictured around 1875, this home is located at Cranbury-South River Road and Route 522. It was built in 1860 by a Mr. Holmes, a New York City businessman. Used mainly as a summerhouse, it eventually became a primary residence around 1870 when J. B. Tollman, another New York businessman purchased the home. When he died in 1885, it was willed to Herbert Brown and his wife, Maria Coley. Later their daughter Gwendalyn and her husband, George Baker Sr., took the possession of the home. Today Sue and George Baker live here with their sons.

THE CLAYTON FARM. Located north down the road from the Baker home on Cranbury-South River Road was Harvey F. Clayton's farm, pictured in 1914. He purchased the farm in 1885. It was partially in South Brunswick and Monroe Townships. Originally the left side was built as a tavern in the 1700s. It was located near Browns Corner (Route 522 and Cranbury-South River Road). It was moved across the frozen farm fields on logs in the mid- to late 19th century. Here Harvey and his is wife, Sara (née McDonald), raised their children, Florence, Elvin, Mildred, Llewellyn, Richard, and Carlton. When Sara died in 1972, the farm was sold.

WHITE EAGLE'S HALL. Standing on the porch on March 3, 1936, are, from left to right, "Pop," Anthony Belluscio, Adam ?, and Philip C. Magrino. At the time, Magrino, shown wearing his uniform, was serving as the first chief of police for Monroe Township. Belluscio was the assistant chief. The township officially created the first police department on March 16, 1935. It was formed as a direct result of the repeal of Prohibition. The hall was located on Bordentown Turnpike near the fork in the road. It was torn down a few years ago, and today 6 and 8 Patio Court occupy the White Eagle's Hall's original site.

PHYSICAL CULTURE CITY. This 1905 advertisement shows some of the local residents swimming in Lake Margurite, named after the city's leader Benarr Macfadden's daughter Margurite. The photograph was taken from the Spotswood side of the dam, facing toward South Shore Boulevard in the Outcalt section of Monroe Township. Physical Culture City disbanded around 1910, and in 1920, the banks were washed away with an ice floe, and the damaged dam was never repaired. Today near the VFW on Daniel Road in Spotswood, this concrete portion of the dam is all that is left.

THE DANIEL ROAD BRIDGE. Locals pose on the newly constructed bridge that crosses the Manalapan Brook around 1920. To the west of the brook about 100 yards, the remains of the dam can be seen from this bridge. The original log bridge was built during the early 19th century. Around 1918, the bridge collapsed while a car was crossing it. Today the new concrete bridge, which was built a few years ago, was raised in elevation from the old bridge due to the flooding problems.

LOG CABIN AT OUTCALT. Built around the time this photograph was taken on January 22, 1930, this log cabin was state-of-the-art for its time. It was located on the corner of Avenue C and Daniel Road. After Benarr Macfadden's Physical Culture City failed, many small summer homes were built in the area. According to the *Outcalt Oracle*, as of August 1925, electricity had not yet come to Outcalt. The article stated a minimum of 12 residents had to commit to the Eastern New Jersey Power Company in order to get power. The cabin was torn down around 1996 by George Bradford. In 1999, a new house took the place of the old cabin at 8 Avenue C.

THE FORSGATE COMPLEX. In 1913, John A. and Alice M. Forster started Forsgate Farms, pictured here around 1950. Around the late 1920s, John became interested in golf. He hired Clifford Wendehack to design a fine clubhouse and Charles Banks to design the 170-acre golf course. The clubhouse was finished in September 1930, and the course opened for play in the early spring of 1931. Invitations were mailed out to 1,000 potential associate members. The dairy farm closed in 1971, and in September 1981, it was announced that the entire complex would be sold by the Abeel family.

THE WORLD WAR II MONROE TOWNSHIP HONOR ROLL. On leave from the army, Monroe Township resident Warren M. Southworth is shown here in September 1944, posing for his fiancée Margaret Eichele (later Daly). He is standing in front of the old wood honor roll that was erected by the Philip C. Marino Association on Anthony Belluscio's property at the fork of Monmouth and Spotswood-Englishtown Roads. Three months later, Southworth was killed on December 22, 1944, during the Battle of the Bulge. He was awarded the Purple Heart and Silver Star posthumously. According to his citation, "a strong combat patrol fiercely assaulted [Southworth's] mortar section from three sides." Southworth "commenced firing upon the enemy . . . for four hours. He then attempted to wipe out an enemy machine gun, but was mortally wounded while creeping up to the position, armed only with hand grenades." Today the old honor roll has been replaced with a stone monument that is dedicated to all veterans.

JAMESBURG

ELLIOT'S MILL, C. 1905. If not for the Manalapan Brook, there might never have been a Jamesburg. Its waters were dammed for the source of steady power in the late 18th century, and a sawmill, a gristmill, and fulling mills had been established on Manalapan Lake. There was a succession of mill owners until, on November 15, 1832, the town's namesake, James Buckelew, purchased the mill and surrounding property. Shown here is Thomas Elliot, who had made his hitherto moveable sawmill stationary. It was located at the foot of Lake Street.

41

LAKEVIEW HOUSE. The original parts of the Lakeview House, pictured around 1910, were probably built in the late 1700s and maybe as early as the late 1600s. On November 15, 1832, James Buckelew took possession of the house, which is presently located on Route 522, across from Dunkin' Donuts. In 1978, the Jamesburg Historical Association saved the home from almost certain demolition. Today it is the pride of Jamesburg. On display in the house is a wonderful collection of Jamesburg and surrounding area artifacts. A recent grant from Middlesex County will help fund a complete restoration.

SHOSTAK'S HOUSE IN THE PINES. The Shostak house was originally built by James Buckelew's son Isaac after the Civil War. Col. Isaac Buckelew was in the Middlesex Brigade of the New Jersey Militia and served in the quartermaster general's department. The house, seen in the 1920s, was built of stone off what is now Buckelew Avenue, between Forge and Lake Streets. Later the mansion was converted into a sort of bed-and-breakfast. It is noted that several famous theatrical stars enjoyed the country setting during their stay. The Tall Tree Apartments and 7-Eleven convenience store now reside where the colonel's estate once stood.

BUCKELEW AVENUE. This image from a glass-plate negative was taken at Buckelew Avenue from Lake Street looking into town in February 1907. To the right, lying along edge of the road, are poles ready to be erected for future telephone and electricity lines. The Monahan's Laundry on West Railroad Avenue (marked No. 1) can be seen off in the distance. Today many of the same houses are still there.

THE FIRST NATIONAL BANK OF JAMESBURG. On January 29, 1864, James Buckelew, with his sons and 20 others, held a meeting at his office and organized the First National Bank of Jamesburg, seen here around 1918. The bank opened in 1864. It served the community well until on July 17, 1926, when it closed its doors at this location for the last time. The institution moved to its newly constructed brick building on West Railroad Avenue and Church Street. Eventually it was torn down when Fred Perrine purchased the property and opened Perrine's Pontiac. Perrine's Pontiac closed several years ago, and here today one will find the Jamesburg Center strip mall.

BUCKELEW AVENUE. This *c.* 1910 postcard view is showing Buckelew Avenue facing east toward Lake Street. On the left is the Lakeview House, and on the right is the First National Bank of Jamesburg. Notice the gas lamps and newly installed telephone and electricity poles. Today the Lakeview House serves as a local museum, and a strip mall is now in place of the old bank.

MANALAPAN LAKE. This *c.* 1908 postcard view by Harry A. Edwards shows five boys and a dog (named Bruce) in a tree on the left as a locomotive approaches from town. In 1851, James Buckelew gave the right-of-way of the stage route to the Freehold and Jamesburg Agricultural Railroad, which he and his son Isaac had established in 1853. The rail line started operation in 1853 and is still used today as a freight route. The last passenger train to use this line was on May 29, 1962. The author's sons, Joseph on the left and Christopher on the right, are seen here standing (minus the dog and train).

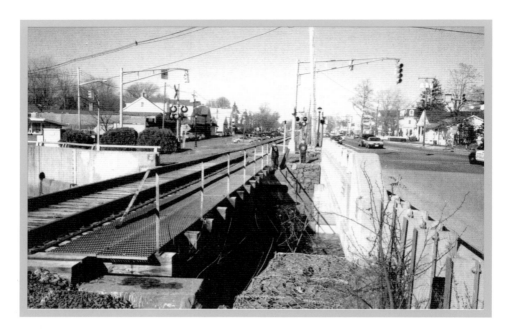

EAST AND WEST RAILROAD AVENUES. This Harry A. Edwards postcard view was taken facing north, at the Manalapan railroad bridge crossing. At the extreme right on East Railroad Avenue is the old William Courter house. Notice how in 1907 East Railroad Avenue was a dead end street, stopping at the Courter/Dreyling Building. Sometime later, East Railroad Avenue was extended to connect with present-day Buckelew Avenue near Dunkin' Donuts. Still visible after 100 years are the huge brownstone blocks of the original retaining wall on which the man is standing.

MANALAPAN LAKE DAM. The old wood dam did not give way during the strong August flood. Beyond the dam can be seen the Westerhoff Brothers, Napier and Company silk mill on August 2, 1906. The mill was built in 1902 by the Jamesburg Improvement Authority. On Saturday afternoon, February 16, 1907, the silk mill burned to the ground. The foundation was reused and brothers Morris and Samuel Shapanka's shirt factory was built there around 1920. In 1926, the shirt factory burned down, and the Kerr's butterscotch factory was built there. Today the concrete dam has long since replaced the wooden dam, and the former butterscotch factory is a professional office building at 300 Buckelew Avenue.

Icehouse and Manalapan Lake Dam. Facing southeast from the dam around 1910, on the left is the huge icehouse nicknamed "Jumbo," built in 1891. It was owned by the Jamesburg Ice Company. It was reported in the *Jamesburg Record* newspaper in January 1893 that this was the best ice harvest ever on Manalapan Lake. Reportedly, as of January 28, 1893, they had shipped 250 railroad cars weighing some 5,000 tons to the shore so far. It had taken 40 men daily to fill all the icehouses including, for the first time, "Jumbo" to a total of 7,500 tons stored. Way off in the distance one can see the former farmhouse of Edmond Rue.

PERRINE'S PONTIAC. Fred Perrine relocated his Pontiac dealership to Buckelew Avenue in the 1940s. Around that time, the old First National Bank, built around 1864, was torn down to make way for the new dealership. The multigeneration car dealership relocated once again around 2000 to Route 130 in Cranbury. The buildings were torn down, and the Jamesburg Center strip mall was built here. Notice the 1947 Pontiac Woodie (center) on the lot.

PENNSYLVANIA RAILROAD LOWER JAMESBURG STATION. With the charter of the Freehold and Jamesburg Agricultural Railroad in March 1851, there became a need of a "lower station." The original station was built around 1857 when the line was opened. In 1913, the lower station was rebuilt and enlarged, as shown here. It was located on the lake, next to the dam. Across the railroad tracks to the left is the Dunkin' Donuts parking lot at the Jamesburg Center strip mall.

MANALAPAN LAKE. Many people, including the author, can remember skating almost every winter on the lake. After the snow was plowed off, the ice thickness was checked by drilling a hole through it. On this day in February 1941, George Houseman measured the ice to be 15 inches thick and safe for skating. In the distance, one can see the First National Bank, painted white by its occupants the Atlantic Service Center. The year 1919 was the last time ice was harvested off the lake.

LOWER WEST RAILROAD AVENUE. This *c.* 1910 postcard photograph by Harry A. Edwards was taken facing West Railroad Avenue and Willow Street. These buildings were constructed on the former site of the Koblenzer and Danzien shirt factory, which had burned down in March 1900. From left to right are the Mancuso Shoe Repair Shop, Cornelious Mounts's meat market, a bakery, and William T. Emmons's poolroom and boardinghouse on the corner. Today Suburban Cleaners, Barber John's, and the Dollar Store are located here.

LOWER WEST RAILROAD AVENUE, LOOKING NORTH. This is a *c.* 1907 view of West Railroad Avenue looking north into town. On the left is a small shirt factory built in 1901 by William Crosby after the big fire that burned down the three-story brick Koblenzer and Danzien shirt factory. The only building to survive the great fire was a residence for the Chinese pressers. This building was converted into John Monahan's laundry. In about 1918, both the laundry and factory were sold to the Shapanka brothers. This factory-laundry combination operated until about 1920 when the Shapankas relocated to their new location at what is now 300 Buckelew Avenue.

WILLIAM T. EMMONS BUILDING. The William T. Emmons building, pictured around 1907, was located on the southwest corner of West Railroad Avenue and Willow Street. It was built around 1905 by William T. "Ginger Bill" Emmons. The building included a bowling alley, a pool parlor, and a boardinghouse. Later in the 1920s and 1930s, the R. Lewis Furniture Store occupied the building. Even later it became Spezio's Grocery Store. Then, on December 23, 1971, the top two stories were destroyed by a fire. It was later rebuilt as a one-story structure. Some of the recent businesses to occupy the building were Jus Subs, Lisko's, and currently the Dollar Store.

LOWER WEST RAILROAD AVENUE STORES.
In February 1907, starting at Church Street toward Forsgate Drive, the following stores line West Railroad Avenue: Fred Grisman's grocery store (1), C. F. Wood's drugstore (2), Fred Kullmar's barbershop (3), C. M. Davison's store, and George VanArsdalen's jewelry store and watch repair shop. The other buildings are the post office (5) until it moved in 1909 to East Railroad Avenue and Church Street, and William T. Emmons's boardinghouse (6). In the distance is the steel bridge erected in 1886 that crossed the Manalapan Brook (7), the lower railroad station (8), and the First National Bank (9).

VETERINARY SURGEON. This is a photograph of the house at 56 East Railroad Avenue as it looked in 1902. At the time, it was occupied by veterinarian Dr. Mark Dier. Dier came from England and settled in Jamesburg. He died there in 1904 at the age of 46. He had three daughters: Myrtle Richards, who settled in Helmetta; Mabel MacKenzie, who settled in Plainsboro; and Beatrice Atkinson, who made Trenton her home. Dier's grave is located in the Fernwood Cemetery in Jamesburg. Today the house is mostly unchanged and has been converted into a two-family apartment building.

No. 58 West Railroad Avenue. This was the residence of Chief William H. Lokerson, as seen around 1905. Lokerson was a charter member of the Jamesburg Fire Company No. 1, which was organized on March 19, 1900. In the program from the department's first annual fair and bazaar (held on April 10–12, 1913), it was said that the department's success at this time belonged to Lokerson, that his heart was in the work, and it was proud to say that every fireman stood loyal to the chief, thus making the members and others feel it an honor to belong to the company. Today the former Lokerson house is a two-family home.

RESIDENCE OF W. H. LOKERSON. JAMESBURG N.J.

Thorburn.

THE MONROE WYCKOFF-ELEVATOR AND FEED MILL. Located at Hillside Avenue and West Railroad Avenue, there were three sets of elevators powered by a 50-horsepower steam engine. Behind the grain elevators, seen around 1914, stood the flour and feed warehouse. Attached to the warehouse was a platform to load and unload the products into the boxcars. By the late 1930s, the mill was abandoned. Long gone is the elevator, mill, and railroad siding that crossed West Railroad Avenue, Hillside Avenue, through the present-day firehouse, and stopping at the former B. D. Davison lumberyard (now Jamesburg Hardware).

No. 42 West Railroad Avenue. Pictured around 1905, this was the residence of George VanArsdalen. VanArsdalen owned the jewelry store and watch repair shop not far from his home on lower West Railroad Avenue. At some point, the house caught fire, and the second and third floors were badly burned. The house was reconstructed to what is seen today. The once beautiful mansard roof has been replaced with a modern gable roof. The house was later owned by the late Sonny Intravatola. Farther down West Railroad Avenue one can see 46 and 47 West Railroad Avenue homes that still stand today.

CONDIT M. DAVISON HOME. The Condit M. Davison home was built around 1910 on the southwest corner of Church Street and Gatzmer Avenue. He was one of the areas earliest real estate and insurance salesmen. He ran his businesses out of his home. Early receipts show he provided all kinds of insurance, such as liability, workmen's compensation, automobile liability, property damage, collision, boiler, engine, flywheel, electrical, accident, health, fidelity, burglary, tornado, and plate glass insurance. Today the Lester Memorial Home, which was established in 1954, occupies the former Davison home.

THE "LINCOLN COACH." Photographed around 1913 is the coach in front of 166 Gatzmer Avenue and Church Street on Decoration Day (Memorial Day). The coach belonged to James Buckelew of Jamesburg and is known as the "Lincoln Coach" because it carried Pres. Abraham Lincoln from the Trenton railroad station to the statehouse where he addressed the legislature in 1861. Today 166 Gatzmer Avenue still stands well preserved and cared for. Notice how many homes have been built and how the trees have matured. The "Lincoln Coach" has been restored and can be seen at the Lakeview House Museum on Buckelew Avenue.

BROOKLAWN. This home, known as Brooklawn and shown around 1890, was located on present-day Forsgate Drive, across the street from the former Jamesburg High School. It is known that in the early 1870s, D. H. Downs of the Downs and Finch Factory built or renovated the old Peter Deremer and Redmond home. On October 15, 1897, Mary and David Kirkpatrick purchased the home and property at foreclosure for $3,000. It was razed in the 1930s. After World War II, David's grandson Malcolm Kirkpatrick and his new bride, Marcia, built the present-day 242 Forsgate Drive home, close to where the old mansion once stood.

HOME OF JUDGE JOHN P. KIRKPATRICK. Judge John P. Kirkpatrick built this fine home, seen here around 1910, next door to his parents' Brooklawn home on the corner of Forsgate Drive and Perrineville Road around 1910. Kirkpatrick graduated from Princeton University around 1900 and later became a Middlesex County judge. The judge died in 1946, and later the house sold to Charles Stoeffler. The last family to live in the house was Mr. and Mrs. Charles DiBrizzi. In 2002, the property was sold to the CVS Pharmacy chain, and the old house at 238 Forsgate Drive was razed in March 2003.

COLLINS BROTHERS SERVICE STATION. This photograph was taken by Harry Housman of Gatzmer Avenue in December 1939. This garage was located on Gatzmer Avenue and Willow Street. The price per gallon of Fire Chief gasoline this day was 15¢. Notice the dead deer hanging from the portico rafters and on the center gas pump being used as Christmas decorations. Just below the huge round Texaco sign is a porcelain sign of a bear saying, "Easy gear shifting this winter." Today the garage has been replaced with the Jamesburg Deli.

VIEW FROM PRESBYTERIAN CHURCH ROOF. This c. 1895 image from a glass-plate negative was taken looking into town facing northeast on East Railroad Avenue. At the upper right is the original Augusta Street School, prior to all the additions being added on. The steeples from the Baptist and Methodist churches are also visible. At the bottom front are some of the church horse sheds. Behind the sheds was the Pineland Incubator and Brooder Company, which was opened in 1887 on Harrison Street by David H. Smith. It manufactured incubators and Fidelity Food for young chicks.

GATZMER AVENUE AND INVERNESS MANSION. This is another *c.* 1895 view photographed off the roof of the Presbyterian church facing north between Gatzmer Avenue and West Railroad Avenue. More church horse sheds are seen at the bottom, and notice the Inverness mansion, the only house to the left of Gatzmer Avenue. The horse sheds were needed for the local townspeople to stable their horses during Sunday worship on days with inclement weather. Today many homes have filled in all the empty lots and farm fields of the former Davison family farm.

GATZMER AVENUE. This *c.* 1910 postcard view was taken by Arway Photo studio facing south on Gatzmer Avenue and Front Street. Not much has changed in the past 100 years. On the corner, 191 Gatzmer Avenue still looks the same, as well as 187 Gatzmer. The only change that seems to have taken place is that the pavement has replaced the gravel road.

B. D. DAVISON LUMBER AND COAL YARD. According to old receipts, B. D. Davison was, in the 1870s and 1880s, partners with Joseph C. Magee. Around 1890, Davison opened his own store. It is shown here at 238 Gatzmer Avenue around 1897. He sold lumber, lime, coal, brick, and building materials. He later sold furniture and was an agent for Ford automobiles. In 1923, the B. D. Davison Lumber Company was sold to Joseph Shaw and renamed Jamesburg Hardware. Wilton Clayton Jr., Shaw's nephew, purchased the store in 1965. His sons Jeff and Gary, pictured here, took over the business in the mid-1990s.

INVERNESS. In the early 1870s, John Dunn Buckelew built a large mansion on a hill north of Half-Acre Road. The main entrance to it was off Gatzmer Avenue where the present Jamesburg Service Center is located. His great-great-grandfather Frederick Buckelew had sailed to America from Inverness, Scotland, in 1715. Because of this, John Dunn called his mansion Inverness, pictured here around 1890. In 1875, John Dunn sold Inverness to his brother Frederick Lemuel. Then his son Frederick Lemuel II and his wife, Mary Elliot, lived in the mansion until Frederick Lemuel II died in 1917. Shortly thereafter, his widow sold the 15-acre estate to a Mr. Chatin. The mansion was destroyed by fire in November 1920 and never rebuilt.

GATZMER AVENUE AND LUMBERYARD. This photograph was taken around 1905 off the railroad bridge facing south toward Lincoln Avenue. The first building on the left is the L. T. Bennet Grocery Store. Formerly it was the original Joseph Magee and James Buckelew lumberyard office, which was established in the 1850s. The next building, which was built around 1900, is the Perrine and Buckelew Lumber Company. Currently the original 1850s office of Magee and Buckelew still stands, but the old Perrine and Buckelew Lumber building was demolished in the mid-1980s. It was rebuilt and today Northeastern Lumber and Millwork Company occupies the location.

CRUGER'S HOTEL. This hotel, seen around 1905, was constructed for James Buckelew on Gatzmer Avenue around 1856 by a Mr. Mount. In the late 1890s, it was purchased by Charles and Maude Cruger. The Jamesburg upper railroad station was located directly behind the hotel. After 30 years of ownership by the Cruger family, it was sold to Alexander Ballantyne. Ballentyne sold it to Earl McFadden, who operated the business until Prohibition. It was torn down in 1944. Around 1949, Ralph and Anthony Busco moved their oil company, Busco Brothers, here. The business is still in operation today where the hotel and railroad station once stood.

STOCKTON STREET. This *c.* 1910 postcard view by Arway Photo studio faces south to East Railroad Avenue. At right is the Monroe Wyckoff-Elevator and Feed Mill Company located on Hillside Avenue. The first house on the left is 7 Stockton Street. Next to it is No. 9. Both homes have been beautifully restored. Across the street is Triangle Park. A new flagpole was recently dedicated to the memory of Henry "Spud" Dobenski for his volunteer work for numerous organizations, particularly his tireless efforts associated with helping veterans in and around the community.

THE VOORHEES HOME. This home was built by Isaac Voorhees around the time he came to Jamesburg as an express agent for the Pennsylvania Railroad, in 1878. He resigned as agent in 1886. That year, his son Milton I. Voorhees became passenger agent. Milton held that position until he retired in 1892. When Isaac Voorhees died in 1899, Milton and his wife, Mae (née Scarlett), relocated from Helmetta to his father's home at 5 Stockton Street, seen here in 1925. Today the home has been converted into the law offices of Otto James Kostbar.

LANGE'S HALL. Otto Lange built this hall on Hooker Street in 1905. Many school functions, such as dances, Halloween parties, graduations, and socials, were held here. In 1909, Lange started showing silent movies at the hall, shown here around 1907. In 1991, the original hall burned to the ground. Soon after, a new home was built in its place at 6 Hooker Street. The first annual fair and bazaar by the Jamesburg Fire Company No. 1 was held at Lange's Hall on April 10–12, 1913. An advertisement in the program from the fair says, "Lange's Hall for dances and shows can be had at reasonable rates."

LANGE'S HA

For Dances a

Shows

Can be had at Reasonable

APPLY AT HAL

P. O. Box 134

OTTO LANGE

BOROUGH HALL AND FIREHOUSE. Pictured around 1907, this building was constructed on Augusta Street in 1898. At this time, the town's one police officer, C. H. Lang, lived on the second floor. There was a two-cell jail on the first floor behind the council room. The unidentified fireman is standing next to the first fire engine of the department. The new Holloway chemical engine was first put on display for Jamesburg to see on July 4, 1900. On that day, a building was erected, then set on fire. When the building was half burned, the engine was put to use and successfully put out the fire. The old building has been replaced by a two-family apartment building known as 7A and 7B Augusta Street.

EAST RAILROAD AVENUE. The stone building, seen around 1925, at 41 East Railroad Avenue was constructed by Frank H. Pownall the same year he established his funeral parlor there in 1882. He did the embalming in his shop, behind the parlor. He also was the owner of the F. H. Pownall Iron Works, established in 1888. Today the building is owned by the Intravatola family and is currently the Hair Parlor Beauty Salon.

THE CORNELIOUS M. FINCH HOUSE. Cornelious M. Finch had this home, pictured around 1907, built on East Railroad Avenue and lower Church Street about the time he came to Jamesburg in the early 1870s. In 1871, Finch and his partner D. H. Downs opened one of the largest shirt factories in the world on lower West Railroad Avenue. They earned over $1 million annually and had over 500 employees. The company went bankrupt in the 1890s, and Finch and Downs left the area. Today the former Finch home is the Jamesburg Dental Center at 29 East Railroad Avenue.

THE WILLIAM H. COURTER HOUSE. In 1850, at the request of James Buckelew, William H. Courter came to Jamesburg to serve as his personal and financial agent. He built his three-story mansion in 1853 on East Railroad Avenue. There he established the W. H. Courter Insurance Agency in 1860. When Courter died in 1901, his grandson William H. Brooks took possession of the home, seen here around 1895, with his mother, Emmeline. Sometime after the death of William H. Brooks in the 1930s, Bill Kerwin purchased the building and insurance business. Currently Roger Dreyling owns both the building and business.

CHAPTER 3

CHURCHES AND SCHOOLS

THE PRESBYTERIAN CHURCH OF JAMESBURG, C. 1869. Early in the 19th century, services were held at the old Jamesburg School on the road to Englishtown, near Schoolhouse Road. In 1847, James Buckelew built a brick schoolhouse and provided a room equipped with a pulpit and seats; a sliding door connected it with the schoolroom. Between 1851 and 1853, a subscription was started for a new church building. The church was dedicated on June 26, 1854, and built on land given by James Buckelew on the corner of Church Street and Gatzmer Avenue. The original building was 45 feet by 38 feet, and a second addition was added in 1867 for 36 more pews at the rear.

THE PRESBYTERIAN CHURCH OF JAMESBURG. In 1871, under the Reverend Benjamin S. Everitt, the third addition took place including a new lecture hall, Sunday school rooms, and room for 25 more pews. The original spire was replaced in 1883 by the present double-towered front. In 1893, the church and parsonage were completely renovated and the new organ, the gift of the Christian Endeavor Society, was installed. In 2006, yet another addition took place at the church. On November 28, 1965, at this church, the author was baptized by the pastor Harold Brackbill.

THE PRESBYTERIAN PARSONAGE. The Presbyterian parsonage was built around 1855 on Church Street, next to the church. Photographed here around 1895 on the front lawn are Emma Heritage's Sunday school children in full dress for a play. From left to right are (kneeling) Tracey Ferris, Bert Paxton, and Cora Harlos; (standing) Raymond Stockton, Jessie Paxton, Harold Paxton, Mattie Lokerson, Roland Stewart, Ethel Davidson (who later married John Kirkpatrick), Edna Westervelt, Mollie Zandt, Edith Paxton, Herbert Stewart, and Bessie Kenzel. Emma Heritage later married the Reverend Benjamin S. Everitt. Today that house remains standing at 9 Church Street.

THE FIRST BAPTIST CHURCH. In 1884, a group of German Baptists of Jamesburg felt the need for a permanent place of worship. They purchased two lots on Stevens Avenue from the Davison estate for $150 each. The structure was partially complete in the fall of 1886 but was wrecked by a terrific windstorm and remained unfinished until the winter of 1887. In 1894, with 55 members, the mission station became an independent church, seen here around 1907. In 1976, the church relocated to its present location on Half-Acre Road. In 1981, the former church was purchased for $100,000 and converted into the Jamesburg-Monroe Senior Center.

METHODIST EPISCOPAL CHURCH. Located on Vine Street, the Methodist Episcopal church, pictured here around 1908, was dedicated in February 1884. By the end of the year, the church was prospering, and in 1904, the mortgage was burned with much ceremony. Under new leadership of the Reverend H. L. Burkett, a new building with nine stained-glass memorial windows, an organ, steam heat, and new furnishings was completed in 1907. On July 27, 1967, the church was destroyed by fire, and the congregation decided not to rebuild. Today Nos. 6 and 8 of the Vine Street Apartments are where the church once stood.

St. James Church. The St. James congregation was organized in 1865. The church was built in 1878 on land donated by a Presbyterian woman, M. C. Buckelew. Seen here in 1907, this church was situated on Lincoln Avenue approximately where the present rectory now stands. This church was demolished in 1957 when the new one was built at the corner of Lincoln and Stevens Avenues that same year. The cornerstone for the present church was laid on September 28, 1958, during the pastorate of Fr. Joseph R. Hughes.

ST. JAMES HALL. The hall of St. James Church was erected in 1885 at the corner of Lincoln and Stevens Avenues, with the front of the hall facing Stevens Avenue. The hall stood until it was demolished in 1949 and the present St. James Church was later built in its place. Groundbreaking for the new church was on August 11, 1957. The blurry image in the 1907 photograph is that of a horse and buggy rushing past the photographer's camera on Lincoln Avenue.

THE UNION VALLEY METHODIST PROTESTANT CHURCH. The plaque on the large boulder monument claims the original Union Valley Methodist Protestant Church was built there in 1790. Then the second church, shown here in the c. 1910 photograph, was built in 1858 across the street on the corner. During the first decades of the 20th century, there was a decline in attendance until finally in 1920 the church closed. In 1925, the last of the remaining old churches of Monroe Township was destroyed by fire. Today the Pondview Plaza is located where the second church once stood.

CHURCHES AND SCHOOLS

THE PROSPECT PLAINS ONE-ROOM SCHOOLHOUSE. Built around 1857, this one-room schoolhouse was located at the northwest corner of the Encore Development on Prospect Plains Road and is pictured here around 1890. It was closed in 1936, when the Applegarth and Barclay Brook Schools were opened. In that same year, it was converted into the first Monroe Township Town Hall. In 1981, the new town hall was opened and the old school was no longer needed. In December 2003, the developer of Encore carefully dismantled the schoolhouse, and it was put in storage until it can someday be rebuilt at the historic Dey farm on Old Church Road.

THE DEY GROVE ONE-ROOM SCHOOLHOUSE. This Monroe Township school was located on the north side of Dey Grove Road close to North Bergens Mills Road. It was built around 1860. At the time of this *c.* 1910 photograph, the teacher was Rebecca Tilton Allen. While she was teaching in Monroe, she stayed with the Kirby Applegate family. She later taught at the Pleasant Grove one-room schoolhouse on Route 33. In 1936, all the one-room schoolhouses were closed when Applegarth and Barclay Brook Schools opened. Today the school is long gone, and the empty lot is owned by the Brenner family of Monroe Township.

THE HALF-ACRE FOUR-ROOM SCHOOL. Located on Cranbury Half-Acre and Union Valley Roads, this school was built in 1907 and was ready for its pupils in September of that year. Shown around 1915, there were four rooms with two grades in each room. Charlotte Ely, a former student of this school, recalled there was no running water in this school. She remembered having to wait until she got home to get a drink of water. That was because the custodian at the school never changed the barrel of water from which the children were to drink. Today this former school has been converted into an apartment building.

THE MONROE ONE-ROOM SCHOOLHOUSE. The Monroe schoolhouse, pictured here in the 1940s, was located on the corner of Route 522 and Schoolhouse Road, where the present-day Central Fire Department is now. The original schoolhouse, built in the 1850s, burned down due to a defective chimney flue in January 1897. It was quickly rebuilt and was painted white. The school was closed in 1936 and on August 8 that same year, it was dedicated as the first Monroe Police Station. In the mid-1970s, it was used as the Monroe Township Administration and Recreation Building. In the late 1980s, it was torn down for the Central Fire Department.

BARCLAY BROOK SCHOOL. Known as school No. 1, the Barclay Brook School is located on Buckelew Avenue in Monroe Township. This photograph on the left was taken on the day of the cornerstone laying. See the "1936" granite stone lying on the ground waiting to be cemented into place. Maria Brown placed the final coat of cement after the cornerstone was set this day. School No. 2 (Applegarth) was built in the same year. Both schools were built with the aid of a Public Works Administration grant at a cost of $150,000. In 1936, there were a total of 14 teachers and 425 pupils. The old school No. 1 has had many additions throughout the years to accommodate the growing student population.

THE AUGUSTA STREET SCHOOL. The Augusta Street School, seen around 1900, was originally built in 1884 as a one-story, two-room brick school. In 1898, it was necessary to enlarge the school. A second floor was added, and if one looks closely, one can see the new addition and the original school. Once again, in 1907, it was enlarged to add five more classrooms. In February 1967, the school succumbed to fire, but from the ashes rose the Grace M. Breckwedel School. It was dedicated on September 28, 1969.

THE JAMESBURG HIGH SCHOOL. In 1927, it was clear that a new high school was needed due to overcrowding at the high school on Augusta Street. The vote was passed after two defeats to construct a new high school on Forsgate Drive, on the former Davison estate. Construction began on the school in 1931, but the class of 1932 did not attend the new school. However, it was able to have its graduation exercise there. In June 1979, the last class of 40 students graduated from high school. On March 22, 1982, the school was purchased at public auction for $200,000 and later reopened as the Forsgate Commons.

ACROSS AMERICA, PEOPLE ARE DISCOVERING SOMETHING WONDERFUL. *THEIR HERITAGE.*

Arcadia Publishing is the leading local history publisher in the United States. With more than 3,000 titles in print and hundreds of new titles released every year, Arcadia has extensive specialized experience chronicling the history of communities and celebrating America's hidden stories, bringing to life the people, places, and events from the past. To discover the history of other communities across the nation, please visit:

www.arcadiapublishing.com

Customized search tools allow you to find regional history books about the town where you grew up, the cities where your friends and family live, the town where your parents met, or even that retirement spot you've been dreaming about.